W9-APJ-066

INFORMATION EXPLORER

SUPER SMART INFORMATION STRATEGIES

# GET READY FOR A WINNING SCIENCE PROJECT

by Sandy Buczynski

CHERRY LAKE PUBLISHING • ANN ARBOR, MICHIGAN

CHERRY LAKE Publishing

Published in the United States of America
by Cherry Lake Publishing
Ann Arbor, Michigan
www.cherrylakepublishing.com

Content Adviser: Gail Dickinson, PhD,
Associate Professor, Old Dominion University,
Norfolk, Virginia

Book design and illustration: The Design Lab

Photo credits: Page 1, ©Ariel Skelley/Glow Images; page 6, ©Monkey Business Images/Dreamstime.com; page 10, ©iStockphoto.com/Bart Coenders; page 13, ©Rmarmion/Dreamstime.com; page 17, ©iStockphoto.com/kali9; page 19, ©Monkey Business Images/Shutterstock, Inc.; page 23, ©Sam Bloomberg-Rissman/Glow Images

Library of Congress Cataloging-in-Publication Data
Buczynski, Sandra C.
  Super smart information strategies: get ready for a winning science project/by Sandy Buczynski.
      p. cm.—(Information explorer)
  Includes bibliographical references and index.
  ISBN-13: 978-1-61080-124-9 (lib. bdg.)
  ISBN-13: 978-1-61080-270-3 (pbk.)
  1. Communication in science—Juvenile literature. 2. Science Projects—Juvenile literature. I. Title.
  Q175.2.B83 2012
  507.8—dc22                          2011002442

Cherry Lake Publishing would like to acknowledge
the work of The Partnership for 21st Century Skills.
Please visit www.21stcenturyskills.org for more information.

Printed in the United States of America
Corporate Graphics Inc.
May 2012
CLFA09

# Table of Contents

# CHAPTER ONE
# That's a Good Idea!

Have you ever wondered how something works?

Are you curious? Are you a careful observer? Do you enjoy solving problems? If so, doing a science project may be just the activity for you!

The goal of a science project is to solve a problem. A science project is an experiment you do or an invention you create to answer a question that you have.

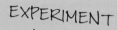
Consider This

## EXPERIMENT
- hands-on activity in the laboratory
- scientific observations of nature
- surveys or questionnaires about issues
- exploration of existing databases

Or This

## INVENTION
- designing and building new devices that can help get certain tasks done
- creating engineering projects
- testing and improving the performance of existing products
- building models to explain what is happening

Experimenters find out things for themselves. Inventors design and make things that will solve problems. Inventors like to think outside the box! Both types of scientists like to collaborate, or work with other scientists who are interested in the same topics.

Where do you find an idea for a science project? How do you find the information you need to understand your topic? Curiosity is the key ingredient! Here are some tips to get you started.

First you need to choose a particular science category to study. This will help you pick the main idea for your project. Decide if you want to experiment with food, plants, chemicals, or something else.

If you are working with a group, make sure everyone helps find a project topic.

# TRY THIS!

## CATEGORIES OF SCIENCE

Take a look at these science subject areas and choose one that interests you.

**BIOLOGY:** anything relating to life, including cells and DNA

**CHEMISTRY:** molecules, acids and bases, solutions and mixtures, chemical reactions

**PHYSICS:** study of matter and energy

**ZOOLOGY:** all about animals in the zoo and in the wild, how they behave and grow

**EARTH SCIENCE:** anything in our environment: rocks, ocean, weather, volcanoes

**ENGINEERING:** desiqning and making structures and machines

**BOTANY:** how plants grow, gardening, seeds

**ASTRONOMY:** stars, planets, the night sky, galaxies, comets, meteors

**FOOD SCIENCE:** healthy eating, burning calories, testing foods, food spoilage

**MICROBIOLOGY:** very tiny organisms such as bacteria, algae, or viruses

**ENTOMOLOGY:** every type of insect, from ants to zebra butterflies

**ECOLOGY:** food webs, plant and animal communities

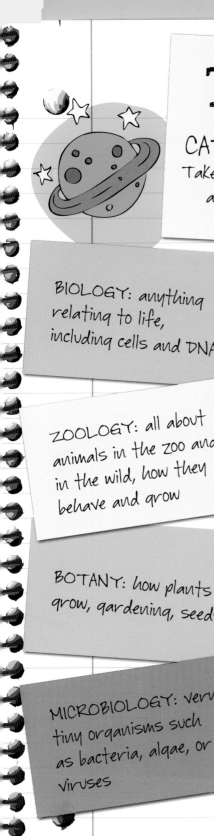

Now you need to research what is already known about your topic. Time to be a detective—library and Internet to the rescue!

Reading about what other scientists and students are studying is a good place to find project ideas.

- Read science news in magazines (*National Geographic World*, *Science News*, *Kids Discover*, *Odyssey*, *Ask*, *Muse*, *Dig*, and many more).

- Read the section of the newspaper that reports science news.

- Look on the Internet for projects that have been done in the past.
  - California State Science Fair
    *www.usc.edu/CSSF/*
  - Science Hound: All Science Fair Projects
    *www.all-science-fair-projects.com/*

- Watch TV shows with science themes (*Bill Nye, The Science Guy*; *MythBusters*; *DragonflyTV*; *NOVA*).

- Find a book on science fair topics.

# TRY THIS!

Once you have a general idea of the areas of science that interest you, visit www.sciencebuddies.org. This site has a feature called "Topic Selection Wizard," which lets you answer questions about your interests. Then it matches you with possible science fair topics.

What topic did Science Buddies recommend for you? Do you agree with this recommendation?

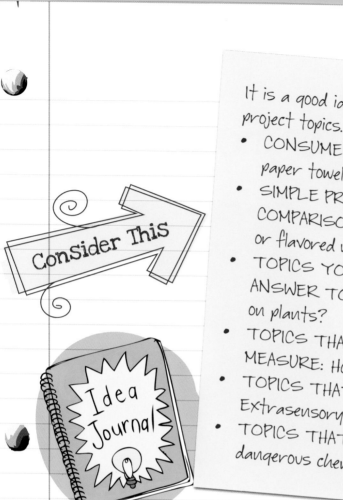

**Consider This**

**Idea Journal**

It is a good idea to avoid some kinds of science project topics. Here are a few examples:

- CONSUMER PRODUCT TESTING: Which paper towel is best?
- SIMPLE PREFERENCE OR TASTE COMPARISONS: Which tastes better, plain or flavored yogurt?
- TOPICS YOU ALREADY KNOW THE ANSWER TO: What is the effect of light on plants?
- TOPICS THAT ARE DIFFICULT TO MEASURE: How does light affect moods?
- TOPICS THAT ARE NOT SCIENTIFIC: Extrasensory perception (ESP)
- TOPICS THAT ARE NOT SAFE: Mixing dangerous chemicals

    Have a journal handy as you explore different ideas. It doesn't have to be a paper journal. You can keep notes on a computer. Inventors, engineers, and scientists all keep written records of their work. Be sure to record the science project ideas that you like the most. You can keep notes on all of the steps you take in getting ready for your science project. This is also a good place to record observations, organize gathered information, and keep track of all of your references. You will need all of this information when you write your background research report.

# CHAPTER TWO
# Find Your Focus

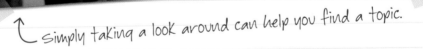

└ Simply taking a look around can help you find a topic.

Science project topics do not have to be complicated to be good. Look over your notes for topics. How can some of those ideas be fine-tuned to better fit your interests? Observation is a great way to focus your science interest. It is one of the most important jobs of a scientist. Observing means using your five senses (touch, sight, smell, hearing, and taste). Observations can jump-start curiosity and give you information about a phenomenon.

# TRY THIS!

Go outside, look around, and ask some questions!

I wonder **how** <u>electric cars</u> work?

I wonder **where** <u>recycling</u> goes next?

I wonder **when** <u>fireflies</u> wake up?

I wonder **what** makes a <u>gecko stick to the wall</u>?

I wonder **what will happen** if I mix <u>yeast and honey</u>?

It's your turn. What do you wonder about? In your science journal, respond to these prompts:

STOP
*DON'T WRITE IN THE BOOK!*

I was really surprised when _____.

I see a pattern in _____.

How are a _____ and a _____ related?
(For example: flower and fruit?)

What is the function of _____?

What might cause _____ to happen?

Still having trouble narrowing the focus of your topic? Try these suggestions:

- Brainstorm out loud with friends, librarians, your teacher, or parents.
- Scan news sites, such as Science News for Kids (*www.sciencenewsforkids.org/*) or Time for Kids (*www.timeforkids.com/TFK/kids*).
- Browse the reference shelves of the library. Look in encyclopedias. Scan the table of contents in science books to find what has already been done on your topic.
- Consider your hobbies or what you like to do in your spare time.
- Think about how to solve practical problems.

## TRY THIS!

Do you have some topic ideas? Great! Now you need to make sure that this is the topic for you. So ask yourself some questions:

1. Does the topic interest me enough to spark my thinking?
2. Is the topic testable in the time period that I have?
3. Will I be able to find the information I need to research my topic?
4. Will I be able to get the tools needed to do the project?

# CHAPTER THREE

# What Is Your Problem?

A good science project starts with an interesting and challenging research question.

Scientists spend a lot of time thinking about their research questions. You must do the same thing. Remember, you need to have a question to guide your experiment or invention process. It will define what you are going to investigate.

A good research question cannot simply be answered with a yes or a no. That is just too easy for a scientist! Scientists usually ask questions that start with how, what, when, where, or which. These questions are clearly written and can be answered with data.

Consider This

Make sure that your research question is clear. It should not be too simple, either.

- UNCLEAR: How can snow stay frozen?
- CLEAR: Which type of material makes the best container to keep snow from melting?
- TOO SIMPLE: What color is an earthworm?
- RESEARCHABLE: How does an earthworm react to light and darkness?

Different kinds of questions can get you thinking in different ways. For example, a measurement question often leads to an answer that is a single number. For this type of question, you might consider what tools would be needed to measure results. You might need a thermometer (for temperature), a meter stick (for distance), a cylinder (for volume), a watch (for time), or a scale (for weight). Measurement questions begin with "how."

A comparison question looks at similarities and differences in results. They let you see how two things are related.

# TRY THIS!

List words related to your topic and then fill in the question blanks with the words!

| Type of question | Possible question starters. (You can think of others!) | Examples |
| --- | --- | --- |
| Measurement questions | How many _____? <br> How long is _____? <br> How often does _____? <br> How hot is _____? <br> How much does _____? <br> How strong is _____? | How often do fireflies blink? |
| Comparison questions | How are_____ and _____different? <br> Which _____is the most effective? <br> How much (longer, heavier, hotter, etc.) is _____ than _____? | Which insulating material is the most effective? |

BLINK!

15

Don't ask questions that

- you already know the answer to
- can be answered with opinions, memories, or impressions (these answers are not factual)
- would require a dangerous experiment to answer

If you can answer yes to these five questions, you probably have a good research question:

- Is the question testable?
- Is the question clear and straightforward?
- Will the question produce data needed to answer it?
- Can you answer this question in a reasonable period of time?
- Is the question safe to answer?

## DID YOU KNOW?

Tools can help you take a closer look at something. Tools used by scientists to observe more closely include magnifying lenses, microscopes, and telescopes.

In 1948, George de Mestral, a Swiss mountaineer, took his dog for a walk. As the dog ran and played, plant seeds stuck to his fur. When he got home, Mestral used a microscope to look at these seeds. He found that they had sharp little hooks. This gave him an idea to create a fastener with hooks like these. Look around. You will probably see this invention on your shoes, backpack, or lunch bag. It is Velcro! It was invented because of one man's curiosity and careful observations.

# CHAPTER FOUR

# Start Your Search Engine!

↳ The library is one place to go to find information.

Scientists build on what has been learned before. This is why collecting background information is so important. You should try to find at least five sources of information about your topic. Let's find out how!

Think of research as a treasure hunt, except no map is given. Create the map yourself as you explore and discover.

- What do I already know?
- What do I need to find out?
- Where should I look for information?

To find your treasure, you can, surf the Internet, visit the library, or interview experts.

The best way to start researching your topic on the Internet is to use **keywords**. Keywords are words or phrases that easily describe your topic. You can input them on **search engines** such as Google and AltaVista, or on subject sites such as Yahoo! A search engine explores Web page databases. It creates a list of sites that will provide you with the kind of information you are looking for. Just as a key opens a lock, keywords open sources of information for your science topic.

**Consider This**

Imagine this research question: How does temperature affect how fast a firefly's light blinks?

What keywords would you use? If you use "firefly" as your keyword, your top hits will include a cell phone service and a TV series. These are not what you want! You can look at the bottom of your results page to find suggestions for other keywords. "Firefly bug" is better! If you type in these two keywords, your top hits include links to an online encyclopedia and science-related sites. They give you descriptions of this little critter and another keyword to use: "lightning bug."

Ask an adult for help if you are not sure a Web site is reliable.

Remember that the Web is a big place, and anyone can post information online. Not all sites have accurate or up-to-date science facts. It is your job as a researcher to make sure that the information you find is reliable. Always try to find more than one source for each fact that you plan to use in your report!

Being able to read a URL (Uniform Resource Locator) helps you judge the value of the information on that site. A URL is the address of a Web page, starting with http:// and followed by a domain name. The name has words in it that tell you what type of site it is. For example, if the URL has ".edu" in it, it is an educational site. These sites are often a good resource.

If a URL has ".gov" in it, it is a government Web site. This is an excellent source for scientific information. The six most popular domain types are:

- .com = this site is commercial; the intent is to sell
- .org = this site claims to be an organization
- .edu = this is a recognized educational site
- .gov = this is a site sponsored by a government agency
- .net = stands for network and isn't specific to one type of user
- .mil = this is a military site

Be sure to double-check the information from sites containing .com (commercial), .org (organization), and .net (network). These sites are unrestricted, meaning anyone can create them.

At the end of the URL address is the "filename," which identifies the type of file you want. The file could be a

- Web page: html, htm
- picture: gif, jpeg
- video clip: mov, mpg
- compressed document: zip
- sound file: wav, au
- word document: doc, docx, pdf

**WHICH IS BEST?**

# TRY THIS!

Which of these .com sites do you think would be the best source for your research on fireflies? Why?

http://animals.nationalgeographic.com/animals/bugs/firefly.html

http://www.trendhunter.com/trends/home-of-firefly

http://www.naturepavilion.com/fireflies.html

If you said the National Geographic site about fireflies would be best, you are correct. Because National Geographic is a well-respected science organization, its site is a good source for the information you need. The Trend Hunter site has a possible idea for an invention but not much scientific information. The Nature Pavilion site is a science gift store.

Many of the sites you find will be blogs or wikis. Blogs are online journals. Wikis are like electronic classroom whiteboards on which anyone can erase information, change information, or add information. Beware! You must judge these sites with the same standards that you use to evaluate any information source.

# TRY THIS!

Now type in keywords on a search engine for your project. Look at the first few URLs on the results page. Use this checklist to decide if these Web sites will be good references for your science project.

What to look for in a reliable Web page

**1.** A TRUSTWORTHY DOMAIN: What type of domain is this site, restricted or unrestricted? Is the content correct?

**2.** AN AUTHOR'S NAME: Look at the bottom of the page. Can you tell who wrote it? Is the author of the page an expert on the topic?

**3.** A RECENT DATE ON THE PAGE: Is the page up-to-date? Look for "last updated" information.

**4.** LINKS THAT TAKE YOU ELSEWHERE: Does the page link to other sites? Do the links work?

**5.** USEFUL INFORMATION: Why was the page put on the Web? To inform? To sell? To entertain?

**6.** A BALANCED PRESENTATION: Is the information one-sided (biased)?

Books are another source of information for your project. Go to your library's computer and enter your keywords in the library catalog. Library books are organized by call numbers. These are numbers placed on a book's spine that tell its location in the library. Track those numbers down to a particular library shelf to find the book you want. On that shelf you will also find other science books on your topic.

Another good source of information is magazines. Magazines are called periodicals because they are published at regular intervals (weekly, monthly, or twice a year). Scientific magazines are called journals. Current journals are kept on shelves in libraries. Older issues

Try looking at magazines and journals to find information on your topic.

are bound in books. You can also check online databases. They may help you locate articles from magazines that your library doesn't subscribe to.

Contacting experts in the field you are studying is another way to gather information. E-mail makes it easier than ever to correspond with scientists. They can be a great source of information, so don't be shy! If you find an e-mail address, go ahead and send the expert a note. These personal contacts might provide you with a primary source—a firsthand account of experiences or events.

# TRY THIS!

E-mail an expert by putting your information in the underlined places in the letter below:

Dear __Dr. Lee__,
My name is __Troy__, and I am a __fourth__ grader at __Seabury__ school in __Vermont__.
I am doing a science project about fireflies.
Would you send me information on __how temperature affects their blinking__?
Thank you for your help.

Sincerely,
__Troy__

No matter what resources you use to obtain information, it is important to make sure that the information is up-to-date, trustworthy, and true.

# RESEARCH CHECKLIST

Make sure you are on the right track.
Did you
☐ combine keywords effectively?
☐ recognize trustworthy sources?
☐ communicate with experts?
☐ collect new and useful information?
☐ keep track of all references in your science project journal?

# CHAPTER FIVE
# Communicate Your Results

Scientists are picky about what they write in their science reports. Only the most important information gets in! Organize the information that you have gathered by grouping related facts together. These groupings become the main headings as you outline your paper.

Writing a science project report is like drawing in the basic features of a treasure map. You fill in your map with details from the explorations of others. This gives you the best idea of the route to follow for your own science research project.

Start the paper with the purpose of your project. What is the mystery that you are going to try to solve? If you are planning an invention, explain why you think your invention would be useful.

Explain any science terms you use. Describe the different parts of the project. For example, if you will be experimenting with fireflies, describe what a firefly is and explain how it lights up. If you are planning to invent a new version of something that already exists, describe the existing product.

## DID YOU KNOW?

It is important to cite, or record, all the places where you obtained information. You include a citation if you:

- use another person's idea or opinion
- quote someone's spoken or written words
- use any facts, graphs, or drawings that are not common knowledge

Sometimes you want to go back and reread an article or recheck a Web site. Be sure to write where you found your information in your notebook, or bookmark the Web page on your computer.

If you write exactly what someone else has said or written, then you put those words in quotation marks. Immediately after the quote, write the last name of the author and the date (Goodlife, 2011).

Your background research report leads you to your hypothesis. What did you learn during your research that could answer your project question? You can pick from these possible answers to form your hypothesis. A hypothesis is a prediction that can be tested. A prediction is what you think is going to happen, but it is not the same thing as guessing! You don't just pluck the prediction out of thin air. Something that you have read or observed guides you to make this prediction.

An "if" / "then" sentence starter can be used for your hypothesis statement.

**If** the <u>temperature is high</u>, **then** <u>fireflies will blink faster.</u>

If your background research report is a sketch of a treasure map, then your hypothesis is your prediction for where the treasure lies. In the end, it doesn't matter if your hypothesis is correct or not. What matters is that it sets you in the direction of discovery. You are now ready to begin experimenting or inventing. Good luck!

## DID YOU KNOW?

At the end of your paper, you need to list all of the references that you cited. Here is how they should look:

- BOOK: Name of author, date. name of book, city, state, publishing company.
- JOURNAL ARTICLE: Name of author, date. name of article, name of journal, volume number, issue number, page number.
- INTERNET REFERENCE: Name of author, title of Web page, date you looked at Web site, URL of Web page.
- PERSONAL CONTACT: Name of expert, date of contact, type of communication, for example: e-mail, phone conversation, letter.

Remember, always list authors with their last names first!

# Glossary

**collaborate (kuh-LAB-uh-rate)** to work with others to do something

**data (DAY-tuh)** a collection of facts or evidence

**databases (DAY-tuh-base-ehz)** sets of collected information that are organized and stored on a computer

**experiment (ik-SPER-uh-ment)** an investigation conducted to test a hypothesis

**hypothesis (hye-PAH-thi-sis)** a prediction about how something works that can be tested with an experiment

**invention (in-VEN-shuhn)** a new device that is created after being tested through experimentation

**keywords (KEE-wurds)** words that can be used to find books, Web sites, or computer files

**observation (ahb-zur-VAY-shuhn)** the act of watching something carefully

**phenomenon (fuh-NAH-muh-nahn)** an event, action, experience, or fact that scientists study

**purpose (PUR-puhs)** the reason why something is done; a goal

**references (REF-ur-uhns-ehz)** books, articles, or Web sites from which you get information to use in a project

**search engines (SURCH EN-jinz)** computer programs that search the World Wide Web for the words you input

# Find Out More

## BOOKS

Truesdell, Ann. *Super Smart Information Strategies: Find the Right Site*. Ann Arbor, MI: Cherry Lake Publishing, 2010.

VanCleave, Janice Pratt. *Engineering for Every Kid: Easy Activities That Make Learning Science Fun*. San Francisco: Jossey-Bass, 2007.

## WEB SITES

**Cool Science Projects**

*www.cool-science-projects.com/*

This site provides resources, helpful tips, and examples to make your project fun.

**Kid Science Link**

*www.kidsciencelink.com/scifairs/index.html*

Find links to many science project and science fair sites.

**Science Buddies**

*www.sciencebuddies.org/*

Visit this site to use the Topic Selection Wizard and the Ask an Expert online bulletin board.

# Index

## About the Author

Sandy Buczynski, PhD, is an associate professor in math, science, and technology education at the University of San Diego in California. She lives in Escondido, California, with her husband, Tony. A big mahalo goes out to her son Troy and his wife, Maria, for their support and help with this book.